LEVEL UP

THE **MINDSET**, **HABITS**, AND **SKILLS** TO BREAK FREE FROM FINANCIAL MEDIOCRITY

Mitchell C. Henderson

Level Up: The Mindset, Habits, and Skills To Break Free From Financial Mediocrity

Copyright © 2024

All rights reserved.

No part of this book may be reproduced in any form without permission, except brief quotations for review purposes.

ISBN: 9798304877398

Disclaimer:

This book is for educational and motivational purposes only. It does not constitute financial advice. Readers should consult a qualified financial advisor before making financial decisions.

This book is dedicated to all who my brothers and sisters

out there who want to break free

from an average life

and excel into

prosperity

Contents

Introduction: Stop Settling for Average	7
Chapter 1: Breaking Free From Average Thinking	10
Chapter 2: Rewriting Your Money Story	14
Chapter 3: Setting Big, Bold Goals	18
Chapter 4: Winning Your Morning, Winning Your Day	23
Chapter 5: Mastering Time and Priorities	28
Chapter 6: Financial Habits for Success	34
Chapter 7: Building Resilience through Discipline	40
Chapter 8: Learning to Earn	46
Chapter 9: Networking for Success	53
Chapter 10: Creating Multiple Streams of Income	58
Chapter 11: Thinking Long-term	64
Chapter 12: Thriving in Financial Freedom	69
Chapter 13: Giving Back and Paying it Forward	74
Conclusion: Level Up, One Step at a Time	79
Bonus Material 1: Action Plan Worksheets	82
Bonus Material 2: Reflection Questions	87

Introduction

Stop Settling for Average

What Is Financial Mediocrity?

Let's be honest. You're not here because you're broke. You're here because you're stuck. You've got a steady paycheck, but at the end of the month, there's not much to show for it. You dream of something better—a life where money isn't a constant source of stress—but the path forward feels blurry at best. That's financial mediocrity: a cycle of just getting by, treading water instead of swimming toward something greater.

Financial mediocrity isn't just about numbers in a bank account. It's the quiet frustration of knowing you're capable of more but feeling trapped by routine. It's working hard every day yet wondering why you're still living paycheck to paycheck. It's being so focused on surviving that you forget what it feels like to truly thrive.

The Cost of Staying Comfortable

Here's the hard truth: comfort is the enemy of growth. Staying in your financial comfort zone—spending as usual, saving only when it's convenient, avoiding the risk of investing in yourself—comes at a high price. It drains your potential, limits your opportunities, and keeps you from the life you were meant to live.

Think about it: how much have you already missed out on because you chose what was easy instead of what was right? Maybe it's the vacation you've always wanted, the freedom to help a loved one in need, or the ability to pursue a dream without worrying about bills. Financial mediocrity robs you of those possibilities—and it's time to take them back.

The Promise of Leveling Up

Here's the good news: you don't have to make massive, overnight changes to break free from mediocrity. Big transformations start with small, intentional shifts. By changing the way you think about money, adopting habits that build wealth, and developing the skills to seize opportunities, you can level up your financial and personal life—step by step.

The promise of this book is simple: if you commit to the process, you *will* see results. You'll stop feeling stuck and start moving forward. You'll turn your paycheck into a tool for growth instead of just survival. And most importantly, you'll finally have the freedom to live the life you've always wanted.

What to Expect in This Book

This isn't your typical finance book. Yes, we'll talk about money—but we'll go deeper than that. Each chapter is designed to challenge you, inspire you, and give you actionable steps to build a life of success and abundance. We'll dive into the mindset shifts that will unlock your potential, the habits that will set you apart, and the practical skills that will elevate every area of your life.

This book isn't just about escaping mediocrity. It's about building a life that excites you, empowers you, and impacts those around you. So, if you're ready to stop settling and start thriving, let's get to work.

The journey to leveling up starts now. Your future is waiting—don't keep it waiting any longer.

Chapter 1
Breaking Free from Average Thinking

The Trap of Comfort Zones

Let's start with a truth that's hard to hear: your comfort zone is holding you back. Sure, it feels safe and familiar, but it's also the reason you're stuck. Settling for "good enough" may keep the bills paid, but it will never help you build wealth, unlock your potential, or create the life you truly want.

Staying comfortable means avoiding risk, sidestepping challenges, and clinging to what's easy—even when it's not working. But here's the thing: real growth only happens when you step out of that bubble. The life you dream about? It's just beyond the edge of your comfort zone, waiting for you to reach for it.

Think about the most successful people you know. Did they get there by playing it safe, sticking to routines, and avoiding discomfort? Of course not. They embraced challenges, took calculated risks, and pushed themselves to do what felt impossible. Breaking free from average thinking means doing the same.

The Growth Mindset vs. Fixed Mindset

The first step to breaking free is changing the way you think about yourself and your potential. Are you stuck in a *fixed mindset*—believing that your abilities, intelligence, and circumstances are set in stone? Or do you have a *growth mindset*—the belief that you can learn, adapt, and improve through effort?

A fixed mindset whispers lies like, "I'm just not good with money," or "I'll never get ahead, so why try?" It convinces you to settle for mediocrity because striving for more feels pointless. But a growth mindset reminds you that change is always possible. It says, "I may not be good with money *yet*, but I can learn." It turns challenges into opportunities and failure into feedback.

The good news? A growth mindset isn't something you're born with—it's something you can develop. Start by rethinking how you approach setbacks. Instead of seeing them as proof that you've failed, view them as stepping stones to success. Every misstep is a lesson, and every lesson brings you closer to your goals.

Exercise: Identify One Area Where You've Settled for Less

Let's put this into action. Take a moment to reflect on your life. Where have you settled for "good enough" instead of striving for more? Maybe it's in your career, where you've stayed in a job that pays the bills but doesn't inspire you. Maybe it's your finances, where you've avoided creating a budget or setting ambitious goals. Or maybe it's in your personal growth, where you've been coasting instead of learning new skills.

Write it down. Be honest with yourself—it's the first step toward change.

Now, brainstorm three small ways you can improve in that area. If it's your career, could you take a free online course or start networking with people in your dream field? If it's your finances, could you set up an automatic transfer to savings or spend 10 minutes a day learning about investing? The key is to choose actions that feel achievable but stretch you just enough to make progress.

Breaking Average Starts with Action

Average thinking keeps you stuck because it convinces you to wait: wait for the perfect opportunity, wait for more resources, or wait for someone else to show you the way. But here's the truth: the perfect moment doesn't exist, and waiting won't change your circumstances.

The only way to break free is to start now. Take one step —even a small one—toward growth. Challenge yourself to think bigger, aim higher, and refuse to settle for less.

Because the life you want isn't out of reach. It's just waiting for you to think beyond "good enough" and go after "great."

Chapter 2

Rewriting Your Money Story

Your Financial Narrative

Everyone has a money story. It's the silent script that plays in the background of your financial decisions. It tells you how to spend, save, or avoid money altogether. This story started long before you earned your first paycheck, shaped by your upbringing, culture, and experiences.

Did you grow up in a household where money was tight, with constant conversations about bills and sacrifice? Or perhaps your parents avoided talking about finances altogether, leaving you to figure it out on your own. Maybe your culture taught you that wealth is a sign of greed or that financial success is only for the lucky few.

Whatever your story, it impacts you more than you realize. If you've ever felt stuck, overwhelmed, or unsure about money, it's likely because the script you're following is holding you back. But the good news is your money story isn't set in stone. You can rewrite it.

Letting Go of Limiting Beliefs

Let's tackle some of the most common money beliefs that keep people stuck:

- *"Money is evil."* This belief has roots in misinterpretations of cultural or religious teachings. Money itself is neutral—it's a tool. What you do with it defines its impact. Money can be used to create opportunities, provide for your family, and give back to others. It's not evil; it's powerful.

- *"I'll never get ahead."* This thought is a self-fulfilling prophecy. If you believe you're destined to struggle, you're less likely to take risks or pursue opportunities. Shift your mindset to focus on what you *can* do today to start moving forward.

- *"I'm just not good with money."* No one is born with financial skills—they're learned. Thinking you're inherently bad with money keeps you from trying. Remember, every financial success story starts with a beginner.

These limiting beliefs aren't facts—they're interpretations. And like any story, they can be rewritten.

Exercise: Write a New, Empowering Money Story

Let's do some storytelling—but this time, you're the author of your future. Start by writing down your current money story. Be honest. What do you believe about money, and where do those beliefs come from?

Now, take a moment to challenge those beliefs. Ask yourself:

- Is this belief helping me or holding me back?
- Where did I learn this belief, and is it still serving me?
- What's a more empowering belief I can adopt instead?

Finally, write your new money story. Make it bold, positive, and forward-looking. For example:

- Old story: "I grew up poor, so I'll always struggle."
- New story: "I grew up poor, which taught me resilience. Now I'm using that strength to create wealth for myself and my family."
- Old story: "I'm terrible with money."

- New story: "I'm learning to manage my money, and every step I take brings me closer to financial freedom."
- Old story: "Money is out of my reach."
- New story: "Money is a tool I'm learning to use wisely to achieve my goals."

Post this new story somewhere you'll see it often—your fridge, your journal, or even your phone background. Repeat it to yourself when doubt creeps in.

Your Story Isn't Over

Rewriting your money story doesn't mean ignoring the challenges you've faced. It means choosing to see them as chapters in a larger journey—one where you are the hero.

You have the power to change the narrative. By letting go of limiting beliefs and embracing an empowering mindset, you'll stop seeing money as a source of stress and start seeing it as a tool for possibility.

This is your moment to take the pen and rewrite your financial future. Your new story starts now.

Chapter 3

Setting Big, Bold Goals

Why Small Goals Keep You Small

Most people live their lives chasing small, safe goals. Saving just enough for the next vacation. Earning just enough to cover bills. Dreaming just enough to feel comfortable—but never enough to feel *free*.

Why? Because small goals feel safe. They don't stretch us too far, don't risk failure, and don't ask us to step outside our comfort zones. But here's the truth: small goals will only ever lead to small results.

If you want to break free from mediocrity, you have to aim higher. Big, bold goals challenge you. They push you to grow, to think differently, and to take actions that scare you—in the best possible way.

Think of the most successful people you admire. They didn't get there by playing small. They dreamed big, took risks, and pursued goals that seemed impossible at first. You can do the same.

The Power of Aiming Higher

Big goals aren't just about achieving more—they're about *becoming* more. When you set an ambitious target, you're forced to develop new skills, habits, and ways of thinking to reach it. The process of growth is just as valuable as the result.

Imagine the difference:

- A small goal: "I want to save $100 this month."
- A bold goal: "I want to save $10,000 in the next year."

The first goal might encourage a few skipped coffees and minimal effort. The second goal? It forces you to think creatively, take on a side hustle, or reevaluate your spending entirely. It changes your behavior, your mindset, and your results.

Reverse Engineering Success

Big goals might seem overwhelming at first—that's normal. The secret to achieving them is breaking them down into smaller, actionable steps.

Think of it like building a staircase. The top of the staircase is your goal. The steps are the actions you take to get there. Focus on one step at a time, and you'll be amazed at how far you can climb.

Here's how to reverse engineer your goals:

1. **Start with the end in mind.** What's the big, bold goal you want to achieve? Be specific.
   - Example: "I want to save $10,000 in one year."
2. **Break it down.** What are the milestones along the way?
   - Example: Save $2,500 every three months.
3. **Identify actionable steps.** What daily or weekly actions will move you closer to each milestone?
   - Example: Save $50 per week by cutting unnecessary expenses, picking up a freelance project, or automating savings.
4. **Track your progress.** Use a journal, app, or spreadsheet to monitor your steps and celebrate small wins.

When you break a big goal into manageable pieces, it no longer feels impossible—it feels achievable.

Exercise: Write Down Three Ambitious Goals

Let's put this into practice. Take a moment to dream big. Don't worry about how you'll achieve these goals just yet—this is your time to imagine the life you want.

1. **Write down one bold financial goal.**
   - Example: "I want to earn six figures within the next three years."
2. **Write down one bold personal goal.**
   - Example: "I want to take my family on a month-long international vacation debt-free."
3. **Write down one bold legacy goal.**
   - Example: "I want to create a scholarship fund for students in need."

Now, pick one goal to focus on first. Write it down somewhere you'll see it every day. This is your target.

Dream Big, Act Boldly

It's easy to settle for average goals in a world that tells you to play it safe. But average won't lead to the extraordinary life you're capable of creating.

By setting big, bold goals and breaking them into achievable steps, you'll start to see opportunities where others see obstacles. You'll develop the habits, mindset, and resilience needed to reach new heights.

Remember: Every big dream begins with a decision to aim higher. Today, you've made that decision. Now, let's take the first step.

Chapter 4

Winning Your Morning, Winning Your Day

The Importance of a Morning Routine

Your morning isn't just the start of your day—it's the foundation for your success. How you spend those first few hours can determine whether you're productive, focused, and energized, or scattered, stressed, and overwhelmed.

Think about this: the most successful people in the world don't leave their mornings to chance. They create routines that set them up to win the day. Why? Because mornings are a blank slate—a chance to take control before life's distractions and demands take over.

When you master your morning, you gain momentum. That momentum carries you through the rest of the day, helping you stay focused on your goals, make better decisions, and show up as your best self.

But it's not just about productivity—it's about *intention*. A powerful morning routine doesn't have to be complicated or time-consuming; it just needs to align with what matters most to you.

Morning Habits for Thrivers

What separates those who thrive from those who merely survive? The answer often lies in their habits. Here are some key morning habits that can transform your day—and your life:

1. **Gratitude** - Start your day with a grateful heart. Take a moment to reflect on three things you're thankful for, no matter how big or small. Gratitude shifts your mindset from scarcity to abundance, helping you focus on opportunities instead of obstacles.

    - Example: "I'm grateful for my health, my supportive family, and the chance to improve myself today."
2. **Goal Review** - Revisit your big, bold goals every morning. Remind yourself why they matter and what steps you'll take today to move closer to them. This keeps your vision front and center, motivating you to stay on track.

- Example: Write down your top three priorities for the day and commit to completing them.
3. **Learning** - Dedicate a few minutes each morning to personal growth. Whether it's reading a chapter of a book, listening to a podcast, or practicing a new skill, starting your day with learning keeps you sharp and inspired.
    - Example: Read 10 pages of a book on personal finance or watch a 10-minute video on investing.
4. **Physical Activity** - Move your body to energize your mind. Exercise doesn't just benefit your health—it boosts your mood, improves focus, and increases resilience.
    - Example: Go for a brisk walk, do a 15-minute yoga session, or try a quick workout routine.
5. **Quiet Reflection** - Spend a few minutes in silence, meditation, or prayer. This helps you center yourself, reduce stress, and approach the day with clarity.
    - Example: Sit quietly with your coffee, take a few deep breaths, and set an intention for the day.

Quick Tips: Create a Morning Plan That Works for You

You don't need to wake up at 5 a.m. or follow a rigid routine to win your morning. The key is to design a plan that fits your lifestyle and sets you up for success.

1. **Start Small** - Don't overhaul your entire morning all at once. Begin with one or two habits and build from there.
   - Example: Start by spending five minutes on gratitude and five minutes reviewing your goals.
2. **Prepare the Night Before** - Set yourself up for success by planning ahead. Lay out your workout clothes, prepare your breakfast, or make a to-do list before bed.
3. **Be Consistent** - Consistency is more important than perfection. Even if you only have 10 minutes, use them wisely and stick to your routine as much as possible.
4. **Adjust as Needed** - Life happens. If your routine gets interrupted, don't stress—adapt. Focus on the habits that are most important to you and keep moving forward.

Winning the Day Starts Now

Your morning is your launchpad. When you take control of how you start your day, you take control of your life.

Imagine waking up with purpose, confidence, and clarity every day. Imagine how much more you could accomplish, how much better you'd feel, and how much closer you'd be to your goals.

That future starts with your next morning. Choose one habit to begin today—just one. With consistency and intention, you'll be amazed at how much your mornings (and your life) transform.

Remember: Win your morning, and you'll win your day. Win enough days, and you'll win your life.

Chapter 5

Mastering Time and Priorities

Stop Letting Time Manage You

Time is the great equalizer. No matter who you are, where you come from, or what you do, everyone gets the same 24 hours in a day. Yet, some people seem to accomplish extraordinary things while others struggle to get through their to-do list. The difference isn't about working harder; it's about working smarter.

Too often, we confuse being *busy* with being *productive*. We fill our days with endless tasks, meetings, and errands, but at the end of the day, we're left wondering if we made any real progress toward our goals. The truth is, busyness can be a trap—a way to feel like we're moving forward when we're actually running in circles.

To level up, you must shift your focus from simply filling your time to *owning* your time. That means prioritizing what truly matters, cutting out distractions, and learning to say no to what doesn't serve your bigger goals.

The 80/20 Rule

Have you ever heard of the Pareto Principle, also known as the 80/20 Rule? It's a simple but powerful concept: 80% of your results come from just 20% of your efforts.

Think about it: not all tasks are created equal. Some actions have an outsized impact on your success, while others are just busywork. When you identify and focus on the activities that drive the most results, you'll accomplish more with less effort.

- **In your career:** What 20% of your tasks bring 80% of your success? Maybe it's closing deals, creating content, or building relationships.
- **In your finances:** What small changes could make the biggest difference? Cutting unnecessary expenses? Increasing your income through a side hustle?
- **In your personal growth:** What one habit or skill could transform your life? Learning about investing? Networking with like-minded people?

Once you identify your 20%, pour your energy into it. Let the rest take a backseat.

Practical Tips for Mastering Your Time

Now that you understand the value of focusing on what matters most, let's talk about how to structure your time effectively.

1. **Weekly Time-Blocking** - Time-blocking is a simple but powerful technique: divide your day into chunks of time dedicated to specific tasks or activities. Instead of letting your day unfold haphazardly, you take control by assigning a purpose to each hour.

    - **Step 1:** Start by listing your top priorities for the week.
    - **Step 2:** Block out time for those priorities first—whether it's working on a project, exercising, or spending time with family.
    - **Step 3:** Schedule everything else around your priorities.

    Example: If you're building a side hustle, block out one hour every evening to work on it. Treat it like a non-negotiable appointment.

2. **Avoiding Distractions** - In today's world, distractions are everywhere—social media, endless emails, and constant notifications. If you're not careful, these time thieves can steal hours of your day.

- **Turn off notifications:** Set your phone to "Do Not Disturb" during focus times.
- **Create a distraction-free zone:** Find a quiet space where you can concentrate.
- **Use the Pomodoro Technique:** Work in focused 25-minute bursts, followed by a 5-minute break.

3. **Daily Prioritization** - Start each day by asking yourself: *What's the one thing I can do today that will make the biggest impact?* Write it down and tackle it first. By focusing on your most important task early, you set the tone for a productive day.

4. **Learn to Say No** - Every time you say "yes" to something unimportant, you're saying "no" to something that truly matters. Protect your time by learning to say no politely but firmly.

   Example: Instead of saying, "I'll try to make it," say, "Thank you, but I can't commit to that right now."

Why Time Mastery Is a Game-Changer

When you master your time, you reclaim control over your life. You stop reacting to what's urgent and start focusing on what's important. Over time, these small changes compound, creating incredible momentum toward your goals.

Imagine a life where your schedule reflects your values and priorities. A life where you end each day feeling accomplished and aligned with your purpose. That's the power of mastering your time.

Exercise: The Time Audit

To start mastering your time, try this simple exercise:

1. For one week, track how you spend every hour of your day.
2. At the end of the week, review your log and ask:
   - What activities added the most value to my life?
   - What activities were a waste of time?
   - How can I adjust my schedule to focus more on the 20% that matters?

Your Time, Your Rules

Remember, time is your most precious resource. Once it's gone, you can't get it back. But by being intentional with how you spend it, you can create a life filled with purpose, progress, and fulfillment.

Start small. Start today. Take back control of your time, and you'll unlock your potential to achieve greatness.

Chapter 6
Financial Habits for Success

Your Habits Shape Your Wealth

Success isn't about one big, lucky break—it's about the small, consistent actions you take every single day. The same principle applies to your finances. It's not just about earning more money (though that's important too). It's about how you *manage* the money you have.

Mastering financial habits is one of the most empowering steps you can take toward leveling up your life. By tracking your spending, sticking to a budget, and consistently investing in your future, you take control of your finances instead of letting them control you.

Let's dive into the habits that will set you up for financial success.

Tracking and Budgeting Like a Pro
Why Tracking Is Key

Ever heard the saying, "What gets measured gets managed"? Tracking your money isn't about restriction—it's about awareness. You can't make meaningful changes until you know exactly where your money is going.

Think of tracking your spending like stepping on a scale before starting a fitness journey. It's not about judgment or shame; it's about creating a baseline.

How to Track Your Spending

- **The Simple Way:** Keep a small notebook or use your phone to write down every purchase for a week.
- **The Tech Way:** Use budgeting apps like Mint, YNAB (You Need A Budget), or your bank's tools to categorize your spending.

At the end of the week or month, review your expenses. Ask yourself:

- Which purchases were necessary?
- Which ones brought value or joy?
- Which ones were impulsive or unnecessary?

Creating a Budget That Works for You

A budget isn't a punishment—it's a plan for your dreams. It's about giving every dollar a purpose, whether it's paying bills, building savings, or enjoying life.

3 Simple Budgeting Methods:

1. **The 50/30/20 Rule:**
   - 50% for needs (rent, utilities, groceries).
   - 30% for wants (entertainment, dining out).
   - 20% for savings and debt repayment.
2. **Zero-Based Budgeting:**
   Every dollar gets assigned a job, so your income minus expenses equals zero.
3. **The Envelope System:**
   For cash-based spenders, use envelopes for different categories like groceries, entertainment, and gas. Once the cash is gone, it's gone!

Pick a method that feels manageable for you, and start small.

Consistent Investing: Start Small, Dream Big

Why Investing Is Crucial

Saving is important, but investing is how you make your money grow. The earlier you start, the more time compound interest has to work its magic. Think of it as planting a tree: the sooner you plant, the more shade you'll enjoy later.

The Magic of Compound Interest

Imagine you invest $100 a month starting at age 25, earning an average return of 8% annually. By the time you're 65, you'll have over $300,000. If you wait until 35 to start, you'll only have around $135,000. That's the power of time and consistency!

How to Start Investing

1. **Begin with Retirement Accounts:** If your employer offers a 401(k) with a match, take full advantage—it's free money!
2. **Open an IRA (Individual Retirement Account):** Choose between a Traditional IRA or Roth IRA based on your tax situation.
3. **Explore Index Funds or ETFs:** These are great for beginners because they're diversified and low-cost.
4. **Use Micro-Investing Apps:** Apps like Acorns or Robinhood let you start with just a few dollars.

The key is to start, even if it's small. $10 today is better than $0.

Practical Tips for Automating Your Success

Automating Savings

One of the easiest ways to stay consistent is to automate your savings.

- **Set It and Forget It:** Schedule automatic transfers from your checking account to your savings account every payday.
- **Create a "Future Fund":** This is your savings for dreams—whether it's a vacation, a new car, or starting a business.

Even $10 a week adds up to $520 a year. The amount isn't as important as building the habit.

Cutting the Emotional Ties to Money

Automation also helps remove the emotional ups and downs of saving and spending. When you don't have to decide whether to save or spend, you're less likely to sabotage your goals.

Exercise: Your First Steps to Financial Success

1. **Track Your Spending:** For the next 7 days, write down everything you spend.
2. **Choose a Budgeting Method:** Pick one of the three budgeting styles mentioned and plan your next month.
3. **Start Investing:** Open a retirement account or micro-investing app and make your first deposit, even if it's just $5.

Why These Habits Matter

Financial success isn't about making six figures (though that helps!). It's about building habits that create stability, freedom, and opportunities. Tracking your spending, sticking to a budget, and investing consistently will set you apart from the majority of people who live paycheck to paycheck.

Each step you take, no matter how small, brings you closer to the life you want. So, start today. Track your spending, automate your savings, and take that first step toward investing in your future.

Your financial freedom starts now.

Chapter 7
Building Resilience Through Discipline

Discipline is Your Superpower

Every successful person shares one essential trait: discipline. It's not talent, luck, or connections that create lasting success—it's the ability to stay consistent, even when things get hard. Discipline is what keeps you moving toward your goals when motivation fades or distractions arise.

But here's the good news: Discipline isn't something you're born with—it's a skill you can build. And the more you practice it, the stronger it gets.

In this chapter, we'll explore why self-discipline is the foundation of success, how to develop it, and daily practices to keep you resilient in the face of challenges.

Why Self-Discipline is the Foundation of Success
The Power of Small Sacrifices

Self-discipline is about choosing long-term rewards over short-term comfort. It's skipping the impulse purchase so you can save for a bigger goal. It's saying "no" to distractions so you can focus on what truly matters.

Think of discipline like a muscle. Every time you choose to stick to your budget, skip an unnecessary expense, or stay focused on your goals, you're strengthening that muscle. Over time, these small choices compound into big results.

Overcoming Temptations

We all face temptations—whether it's binge-watching a show instead of working on a side hustle or buying something you don't need because it's on sale. Discipline isn't about never being tempted; it's about building the strength to say "no" when those temptations arise.

Ask yourself:

- Will this choice bring me closer to my goals, or take me further away?
- Is this a need or a want?
- How will I feel about this decision tomorrow?

Daily Practices to Stay Disciplined
1. Start Your Day with Affirmations

Affirmations are positive statements that remind you of your purpose and goals. They set the tone for your day and keep your mind focused on what matters most.

Try these affirmations:

- "I am disciplined and focused on my goals."
- "I make choices that align with my dreams."
- "I have the power to create the life I want."

Write your affirmations down or say them out loud every morning to ground yourself in your intentions.

2. Use Accountability Partners

Accountability is a powerful motivator. When someone else knows your goals, you're more likely to stay committed.

Here's how to leverage accountability:

- Share your financial or personal goals with a trusted friend, family member, or mentor.
- Check in regularly to update them on your progress.
- Be honest about your struggles—they're there to support you, not judge you.

Many people find success in group settings like online communities or mastermind groups where everyone works toward similar goals.

3. Reflect on Your Progress

Reflection helps you stay disciplined by reminding you of how far you've come. It's easy to get discouraged when you focus on what's still ahead, but looking back at your progress can reignite your motivation.

Daily or weekly, take a few minutes to ask yourself:

- What did I do well today?
- Where did I struggle?
- What can I do differently tomorrow?

Reflection isn't about beating yourself up—it's about learning and growing.

Exercise: Build Your Discipline Plan

1. **Identify an Area to Improve** - Think about a habit or behavior where you struggle with discipline. It could be overspending, procrastinating, or skipping your daily routine.

2. **Set a Clear Goal** - What do you want to change or achieve? Be specific. Instead of saying, "I want to save money," say, "I want to save $100 this month by eating out less."

3. **Create a Step-by-Step Plan** - Break your goal into manageable actions. For example:

- Step 1: Track how much I spend on dining out each week.
- Step 2: Set a weekly budget for dining out and stick to it.
- Step 3: Cook three meals at home instead of eating out.

4. **Build Accountability** - Tell a friend or family member about your goal and ask them to check in with you.
5. **Reflect Regularly** - Review your progress at the end of each week. Celebrate your wins and adjust your plan as needed.

The Long-Term Benefits of Discipline

Discipline doesn't just help you achieve your financial and personal goals—it transforms who you are. Every time you choose discipline over comfort, you build confidence, resilience, and self-respect. You prove to yourself that you're capable of doing hard things and sticking to your word.

In the end, it's not about perfection. It's about persistence. Even if you slip up, get back on track and keep moving forward. Success isn't about never falling—it's about always getting back up.

Remember: Every small, disciplined choice you make today brings you closer to the life you've always dreamed of. Start building that resilience now. Your future self will thank you.

Chapter 8
Learning to Earn

Your Most Valuable Asset: You

If you could invest in one thing guaranteed to grow your income, open doors, and give you greater control over your financial future, wouldn't you jump at the opportunity? That investment is you. Your knowledge, skills, and expertise are your most valuable assets, and when you commit to improving them, your earning potential skyrockets.

In today's fast-changing world, staying stagnant is not an option. The good news? Learning to earn isn't about going back to school for years or spending a fortune on training. It's about being strategic, identifying high-value skills, and using the countless free and affordable resources available today to level up.

This chapter is all about investing in yourself, building skills that demand higher pay, and positioning yourself to thrive in any economy.

Why Upskilling is Non-Negotiable
The Economy is Changing—Fast

Technology, globalization, and automation are reshaping industries at lightning speed. Skills that were valuable five years ago might be outdated today. The ability to adapt and learn new skills isn't just a nice-to-have—it's a survival skill.

But don't let that intimidate you. Think of this as an opportunity. By proactively learning and growing, you can stay ahead of the curve and create opportunities for yourself instead of waiting for them to appear.

More Skills = More Income

Every skill you add to your toolbox increases your value in the marketplace. Whether it's learning a technical skill like coding, mastering a trade, or improving soft skills like communication, every new ability makes you more competitive and opens doors to higher-paying opportunities.

Confidence Comes from Competence

One of the hidden benefits of upskilling is the confidence it brings. The more you learn, the more capable you feel—and that confidence can translate into bold career moves, better negotiation, and greater income.

Identifying High-Income Skills

Not all skills are created equal. To maximize your earning potential, focus on building what are often called "high-income skills"—skills that are in demand, adaptable to different industries, and capable of generating significant income.

Here are a few examples:

- **Technical Skills**: Coding, data analysis, digital marketing, graphic design.
- **Sales and Persuasion**: The ability to sell products, services, or ideas is always valuable.
- **Leadership and Management**: Leading teams effectively can open doors to higher-paying roles.
- **Communication and Public Speaking**: Strong communication skills can set you apart in any field.
- **Creative Skills**: Content creation, photography, or video editing can lead to freelance or entrepreneurial opportunities.

How to Choose the Right Skills for You

- **Look at Demand**: Research which skills are in demand in your field or industry.
- **Leverage Your Interests**: What excites you? Learning is easier when you're passionate about the subject.

- **Consider the ROI**: Focus on skills that can significantly increase your earning potential.

Resources for Continuous Learning

You don't need to spend thousands of dollars to learn new skills. In fact, some of the best resources are free or very affordable. Here's where to start:

Online Platforms

- **Coursera and edX**: Access courses from top universities, often for free.
- **Udemy and Skillshare**: Affordable courses on a wide range of skills, from coding to graphic design.
- **LinkedIn Learning**: Professional courses tailored to career development.

Free Tools and Resources

- **YouTube**: A goldmine of tutorials and how-to videos.
- **Khan Academy**: Free, high-quality education on various subjects.
- **Local Libraries**: Many libraries offer free access to online courses, books, and resources.

Practical Learning Opportunities

- **Volunteer or Freelance**: Gain experience while building your skills.
- **Mentorship**: Learn from someone who's already successful in your desired field.
- **Workshops and Meetups**: In-person or virtual events can provide hands-on experience and networking opportunities.

Daily Practices to Build Your Skills

Dedicate Time to Learning

Start small—commit just 15-30 minutes a day to learning something new. Over time, these small increments add up to a wealth of knowledge.

Practice, Don't Just Consume

It's not enough to watch tutorials or read books—you need to put your skills into action. Build projects, take on small gigs, or find ways to apply what you're learning in your current job.

Track Your Progress

Keep a journal or spreadsheet of the skills you're working on and the milestones you've achieved. Seeing how far you've come is incredibly motivating.

Exercise: Build Your Learning Plan

1. **Choose One Skill** - Pick a skill that excites you and aligns with your financial goals.

2. **Set a Timeline** - Decide how long you'll dedicate to learning and practicing this skill.

3. **Find Your Resources** - List the books, courses, or tools you'll use to learn.

4. **Practice Consistently** - Block out time in your daily or weekly schedule to practice.

5. **Measure Your Progress** - Set benchmarks, like completing a course or landing your first freelance gig, to track your growth.

The Long-Term Payoff of Learning to Earn

Investing in yourself isn't just about money—it's about freedom. When you have valuable skills, you create options for yourself. You can change careers, start a business, negotiate a higher salary, or turn a side hustle into a full-time income.

Every time you learn something new, you're leveling up your potential. The skills you build today will pay dividends for years to come.

Remember: Your ability to learn and adapt is your greatest asset. Start investing in yourself today, and watch as the doors of opportunity swing wide open.

Chapter 9
Networking for Success

Your Network is Your Net Worth

If you want to go fast, go alone. If you want to go far, go together. Success is rarely a solo journey. Behind every thriving person is a network of people who inspired, supported, challenged, and guided them along the way. Relationships are the currency of success, and the people you surround yourself with have the power to shape your future.

The truth is, who you know matters—but not in the shallow, transactional sense that networking sometimes implies. True networking is about building meaningful connections, sharing value, and creating a circle of people who push you to grow and thrive.

Whether you're looking to advance in your career, start a business, or simply level up in life, building the right relationships is a game-changer. In this chapter, we'll explore how to cultivate a network that fuels your success, even if you're naturally introverted or feel intimidated by the idea of networking.

Why Relationships Matter More Than Ever

Opportunities Come Through People

The best opportunities often come through referrals, recommendations, and relationships. That dream job, investment opportunity, or partnership isn't just floating in the ether—it's likely in the hands of someone in your network (or someone they know).

Mentorship Accelerates Growth

Learning from others' experiences is one of the fastest ways to grow. A good mentor can help you avoid pitfalls, see opportunities you might overlook, and guide you through challenges with wisdom born from experience.

Community Fuels Motivation

Surrounding yourself with driven, growth-oriented individuals creates a ripple effect. When you're part of a circle where ambition, positivity, and success are the norm, it raises your standards and inspires you to aim higher.

Building a Growth-Oriented Circle

Who Should Be in Your Circle?

To create a network that elevates you, aim to include:

- **Mentors**: People who've achieved what you aspire to and can guide you.
- **Peers**: Those on a similar journey who can share insights and keep you accountable.
- **Supporters**: Friends, family, or colleagues who cheer you on and believe in your potential.

Where to Find These People

- **Professional Events**: Attend conferences, seminars, and industry meetups.
- **Online Communities**: Join LinkedIn groups, forums, or social media communities aligned with your interests.
- **Classes and Workshops**: Learning environments are perfect for meeting growth-minded individuals.
- **Volunteering or Clubs**: Shared interests and causes can create genuine connections.

Practical Tips for Networking

Start by Adding Value

Networking isn't about asking, "What can I get from this person?" It's about asking, "How can I help them?"

Whether it's sharing resources, making an introduction, or simply offering encouragement, leading with value creates a foundation of trust and goodwill.

Be Genuine
People can sense when you're being inauthentic. Focus on building real relationships based on mutual respect and shared interests, not just what someone can do for you.

Be Proactive
Don't wait for others to come to you. Reach out, follow up, and take the initiative to maintain connections. A simple message or coffee invitation can go a long way in keeping relationships alive.

For Introverts: Networking Your Way
If large events and small talk make you cringe, that's okay. Focus on one-on-one interactions or smaller gatherings where you can build deeper connections. Online networking can also be a great way to ease into building relationships.

Exercise: Expanding Your Network
1. **List Your Current Network**
   Write down the names of people you already know who inspire, support, or challenge you.

2. **Identify Gaps**
   Are you missing mentors, peers, or supporters in specific areas? Identify the types of people you'd like to connect with.

3. **Take Action**
   Reach out to one person this week—whether it's rekindling an old connection, introducing yourself to someone new, or asking for advice.

4. **Commit to Consistency**
   Set a goal to connect with at least one new person each month. Over time, these small actions build a powerful network.

The Ripple Effect of Relationships

Every meaningful connection has the potential to change your life. But the beauty of networking is that it's not just about what you gain—it's about what you give. When you build authentic relationships and invest in others, you create a ripple effect of growth and success that impacts everyone involved.

Remember, it's not about knowing everyone. It's about knowing the right people—the ones who lift you higher, challenge you to grow, and inspire you to keep leveling up.

Your network is waiting. Start building it today.

Chapter 10

Creating Multiple Streams of Income

Why One Income Isn't Enough

Relying on a single paycheck is like standing on a one-legged stool—one misstep, and it all comes crashing down. In today's uncertain world, depending solely on one income stream puts your financial stability at risk. What if you lose your job? What if unexpected expenses arise?

The most successful people don't just rely on one source of income; they build multiple streams. Each stream acts like an additional leg on that stool, providing more balance and security. This isn't about chasing the next get-rich-quick scheme. It's about creating sustainable, diverse sources of income that can support you in any season of life.

Imagine having income flowing in from multiple places—money working for you, even while you sleep. It's not a dream; it's a mindset and strategy anyone can adopt, starting today.

The Power of Diversification

When you diversify your income, you're not just protecting yourself—you're setting yourself up for growth. Each new stream is a step closer to financial freedom. Here's why multiple streams of income matter:

1. **Security**: If one stream dries up, you have others to fall back on.
2. **Opportunities**: More income allows you to invest in your future.
3. **Freedom**: You're no longer tied to a single source or employer.

The good news? You don't need to be rich or an expert to start building multiple streams of income. You just need a plan and the willingness to take small, consistent steps.

Side Hustles: Turning Time into Money

A side hustle is one of the fastest ways to create an additional income stream. It's about leveraging your skills, interests, or spare time to generate money beyond your primary job.

Popular Side Hustle Ideas:

- **Freelancing**: Use your skills in writing, graphic design, coding, or consulting.
- **Selling Products**: Open an online store or sell handmade goods on platforms like Etsy.
- **Service-Based Work**: Offer tutoring, pet sitting, cleaning, or other services in your community.
- **Driving or Delivery**: Sign up for ride-share or food delivery services.
- **Online Teaching**: Share your knowledge by teaching courses on platforms like Udemy or Skillshare.

Pro Tip: Start with something low-risk. Choose a hustle that requires minimal upfront investment and aligns with your skills or interests.

Passive Income: Make Money While You Sleep

Passive income is the holy grail of financial freedom. It's money that flows in with little to no daily effort once it's set up. While it often requires some upfront work or investment, the rewards can be life-changing.

Passive Income Ideas:

- **Investments**: Stocks, bonds, or real estate that generate returns over time.

- **Digital Products**: Write an eBook, create a course, or sell stock photos.
- **Affiliate Marketing**: Promote products you believe in and earn a commission on sales.
- **Rental Income**: Rent out a property, a room, or even equipment.
- **Royalties**: Earn from creative work like books, music, or patents.

Getting Started: Choose one area to focus on and take small, deliberate steps. For example, start with a savings goal for your first investment or dedicate weekends to building a digital product.

Practical Steps to Build Multiple Streams

Step 1: Assess Your Skills and Interests
What are you good at? What do you enjoy? Look for opportunities that align with your strengths and passions.

Step 2: Start Small
Begin with one side hustle or passive income idea. Once it's running smoothly, add another.

Step 3: Automate When Possible
For passive income, automation is key. Set up systems to manage investments, sales, or marketing so you can focus on scaling.

Step 4: Reinvest Earnings

Use the income from one stream to fund or grow another. For instance, profits from a side hustle can go toward investments.

Step 5: Stay Consistent

Building multiple streams takes time. The key is persistence and gradual progress.

Exercise: Brainstorm Your Streams

Take a moment to map out potential income streams:

1. **Skill-Based Ideas**: What talents or knowledge can you monetize?
2. **Time-Based Ideas**: What services could you offer in your spare time?
3. **Investment-Based Ideas**: Where could you start investing for long-term returns?

Choose one idea and commit to taking the first step this week—whether it's researching the market, creating a plan, or signing up for a platform.

Your Future, Powered by Multiple Streams

Imagine this: It's a year from now. You're earning from not just one, but two or three streams of income. You're saving more, investing more, and feeling a sense of security and freedom you've never had before.

It all starts with one step. Building multiple streams of income isn't reserved for the wealthy—it's a strategy anyone can adopt. It's your key to breaking free from financial limitations and designing a life of abundance.

The question is: Which stream will you start building today?

Chapter 11
Thinking Long-Term

The Importance of Vision

If you're constantly focused on today—just paying bills, surviving the week, or chasing quick wins—you'll never unlock your full potential. Thriving in life requires more than just solving immediate problems; it demands vision. Vision is your ability to see the bigger picture of your life and aim for something greater.

Think about it: every great achievement started with a clear vision. Entrepreneurs build empires because they can see possibilities beyond the present. Athletes train relentlessly because they visualize themselves holding that championship trophy. Vision gives you a reason to push forward, even when the journey gets tough.

The problem is, most people live day-to-day. They're so busy reacting to life that they never stop to ask:

- Where do I want to be in five years?
- What do I want my future to look like?

Without vision, you stay stuck in the cycle of mediocrity. With vision, you chart a course toward a thriving, abundant future.

Think Bigger, Think Further

Short-term thinking can feel rewarding in the moment, but it rarely leads to lasting success. Long-term thinking, on the other hand, helps you focus on what truly matters.

Here's why long-term thinking is critical:

1. **It Gives You Direction**: When you know your destination, every decision becomes clearer.
2. **It Builds Patience**: You're less likely to chase instant gratification when you have a bigger goal in mind.
3. **It Maximizes Results**: Long-term planning allows time for small efforts to compound into extraordinary results.

Imagine your life five years from now. What do you want to have accomplished financially, personally, and professionally? That vision can act as your north star, guiding your choices every single day.

The Power of Compound Growth

Albert Einstein once called compound interest the "eighth wonder of the world." He wasn't just talking about money—he was talking about how consistent, small actions lead to exponential growth over time.

In Finances:
When you save or invest even small amounts consistently, the power of compounding turns those efforts into significant wealth. A single dollar saved today can grow into ten dollars tomorrow and a hundred dollars years down the line. The earlier you start thinking long-term, the greater the payoff.

In Skills:
The same principle applies to personal growth. Spending just 15 minutes a day learning a new skill might not seem life-changing at first, but over a year, it adds up to 91 hours of focused growth. In five years, you could master a skill that transforms your career or business.

Success is not about doing one big thing; it's about doing the right small things consistently over time.

Practical Tips for Long-Term Thinking

1. Start with a Vision:
What kind of life do you want to live five years from now? Visualize every detail—your finances,

relationships, career, and personal growth. Write it down. This is your roadmap.

2. Break It Down:
Once you have your vision, break it into smaller milestones. For example:

- Year 1: Save $5,000, complete a certification, and reduce debt by 25%.
- Year 2: Start a side hustle, grow your investments, and improve your networking skills.

3. Focus on Systems, Not Just Goals:
Goals are great for direction, but systems are what keep you on track daily. A goal might be to save $50,000 in five years. The system is automating your savings and tracking your progress monthly.

4. Stay Adaptable:
Long-term thinking doesn't mean rigid thinking. Life will throw curveballs, and that's okay. Adjust your plan, but never lose sight of the big picture.

Exercise: Create Your Five-Year Vision

Take 20 minutes to complete this exercise. Imagine it's five years from today:

1. **Financially**: How much do you want to have saved, invested, or earned?

2. **Professionally**: What skills, achievements, or roles do you want to have?
3. **Personally**: What kind of relationships, health, and lifestyle do you want to enjoy?
4. **Experiences**: What adventures, travels, or milestones do you want to celebrate?

Write it all down in vivid detail. Don't hold back—dream big.

Living for Tomorrow, Starting Today

Thinking long-term isn't just about planning—it's about becoming. Each small action you take today is a vote for the person you'll be tomorrow. Every dollar you save, every book you read, every step you take toward your vision is proof that you're not settling for average.

It's easy to stay comfortable. It's harder to think beyond the moment. But the rewards? They're life-changing.

In five years, you could be living a life you once thought impossible. And it all starts with a choice: Will you settle for the immediate, or will you invest in the extraordinary future waiting for you?

The decision is yours. Choose to think long-term. Choose to thrive.

Chapter 12

Thriving in Financial Freedom

What Does Thriving Look Like?

Thriving is more than having enough money to pay the bills or splurge on a vacation—it's living a life of true abundance, security, and impact. When you're thriving financially, money becomes a tool to create opportunities, enjoy peace of mind, and make a difference in the world.

Imagine waking up without the weight of financial stress pressing on your chest. You're not just surviving or getting by—you're in control. You have the freedom to choose how you spend your time, where you work, and what dreams you pursue. That's the power of financial freedom.

Thriving isn't about having millions in the bank (though that doesn't hurt); it's about reaching a point where money works for you rather than the other way around.

It's living life with purpose and knowing you've built a foundation that allows you to weather storms, seize opportunities, and leave a lasting legacy.

Practical Financial Milestones

To thrive financially, you need a plan with clear, achievable milestones. Here are three core elements of financial freedom:

1. **Emergency Fund**:
   An emergency fund is your safety net. It shields you from life's unexpected expenses, like medical bills, car repairs, or sudden job loss. A solid emergency fund should cover 3–6 months of living expenses. It's not about luxury; it's about security.

   Action Step: If you haven't started yet, build a $1,000 cushion. Then, grow it until you reach the full 3–6 months of expenses. Automate contributions to make it easier.

2. **Zero Debt**:
   Debt keeps you tied to the past. Whether it's credit cards, student loans, or car payments, every dollar spent on debt is a dollar that could be working for your future. Imagine the freedom of living without monthly payments draining your income.

Action Step: Focus on eliminating high-interest debt first. Use the snowball or avalanche method to tackle balances systematically. Celebrate every victory—paying off even one small debt is a step toward freedom.

3. **Growing Investments**:
   Thriving means your money works as hard as you do. Investments are the key to building long-term wealth. Whether it's a 401(k), IRA, real estate, or a diversified portfolio, every dollar you invest today has the potential to multiply over time.

   Action Step: Commit to investing regularly, even if it's a small amount. Use compound growth to your advantage, and don't let market ups and downs derail your plan.

Thriving Beyond Money

Financial freedom isn't just about numbers—it's about the life those numbers make possible. Thriving looks different for everyone, but it often includes:

- **Peace of Mind**: Knowing you're prepared for the unexpected.
- **Time Freedom**: Spending your time on what matters most to you, not just earning a paycheck.

- **Generosity**: Having the ability to give freely to causes, people, and communities that inspire you.
- **Opportunities**: Pursuing passions, learning new skills, or taking risks without fear of financial ruin.

It's not just about getting ahead—it's about staying ahead and lifting others along the way.

Reflection: Imagine Your Life Thriving

Take a moment to close your eyes and imagine your thriving life. Where are you living? What does your day look like? What are you doing that fills your life with purpose and joy?

Picture yourself:

- Waking up in a home you love, debt-free and secure.
- Opening your banking app to see a growing balance in your investment accounts.
- Traveling to new places, helping loved ones, or funding projects that make a difference.
- Sleeping soundly at night, knowing you've built a legacy for your future.

Thriving is within reach. Every step you've taken through this book has been leading to this moment.

The Journey to Thriving

You don't have to wait until you hit every financial milestone to start thriving. The truth is, thriving begins the moment you decide to take control of your life and your money. Each small habit, each bold goal, each disciplined choice brings you closer to the freedom and abundance you desire.

Remember: thriving isn't a finish line—it's a mindset. It's the courage to dream big and the discipline to take small steps every day. It's living with intention and knowing you're on a path to something extraordinary.

You've come so far. Keep going. Your best life is ahead of you, waiting to be claimed.

Now, take a deep breath, look forward, and step boldly into your thriving future. The world is yours to conquer.

Chapter 13
Giving Back and Paying It Forward

The Joy of Generosity

There's a secret many wealthy and thriving people know: true abundance doesn't come from keeping—it comes from giving. Generosity isn't just about writing a check or donating to charity; it's about embracing a mindset that says, "I have enough to share."

When you give back, whether it's with your money, time, or skills, you create a ripple effect that transforms lives—starting with your own. Studies show that acts of generosity increase happiness, reduce stress, and even improve physical health. But beyond the science, there's something deeply fulfilling about knowing you've made someone's life better.

Generosity rewires your brain to focus on abundance. Instead of dwelling on what you lack, you begin to see and appreciate all you've gained. The act of giving shifts your perspective: it reminds you of how far you've come and inspires you to keep reaching higher—not just for yourself but for the people who will benefit from your success.

Mentoring Others

Your journey to break free from financial mediocrity and thrive has not only equipped you to succeed but also positioned you to help others. Mentoring someone who's just starting out, sharing your story, or teaching financial habits you've mastered can make a world of difference for someone feeling stuck.

Mentorship doesn't have to be formal or overwhelming. It could mean:

- Offering advice to a younger colleague who's just beginning their career.
- Sharing budgeting tips with a friend struggling to get ahead.
- Volunteering to teach financial literacy in your community.
- Simply being a listening ear for someone trying to take their first steps toward leveling up.

When you mentor others, you solidify your own growth. Teaching what you've learned reinforces those lessons in your life and helps you stay grounded in the principles that brought you success.

The Ripple Effect of Giving

Every act of giving creates a ripple effect. That small act of kindness, guidance, or generosity can grow exponentially as it touches others. When you give, you're not just changing one life—you're inspiring others to give, creating a cycle of abundance that stretches far beyond what you can see.

Think about the people who inspired you. Maybe it was a teacher who encouraged you to dream bigger, a family member who showed you the value of hard work, or a mentor who believed in you when you didn't believe in yourself. Their impact on your life is proof of the power of paying it forward.

Now, it's your turn.

Reflection: What Legacy Do You Want to Leave Behind?

The question of legacy is one of the most powerful reflections you can undertake. When you think about the end of your life, how do you want to be remembered? What kind of impact do you want to leave behind?

Imagine this:

- Your children or loved ones thriving because you taught them financial wisdom and provided opportunities.
- Your community stronger because of your contributions and generosity.
- Strangers whose lives were improved because of the organizations or causes you supported.

Legacy isn't about being famous or leaving behind vast sums of money. It's about the difference you make in the lives you touch. It's about knowing that your success was never just about you—it was about paving the way for others to rise as well.

Start Giving Back Today

Generosity doesn't require perfection. You don't have to wait until you're debt-free or have thousands in the bank to give back. Start small:

- Donate $5 to a cause you care about.
- Volunteer an hour of your time this week.
- Share a tip, a resource, or an encouraging word with someone in need.

Remember, generosity is a muscle. The more you exercise it, the stronger it becomes. Over time, giving will feel as natural as breathing—and it will bring you unparalleled joy.

The Joy of Full Circle

When you've climbed a mountain, there's nothing more rewarding than reaching back to help someone else begin their ascent. Giving back isn't the end of your journey—it's the next level. It's the part of thriving that brings your success full circle, connecting your achievements with a greater purpose.

You've worked hard to get to where you are. Now, let your success be a beacon for others. Show them what's possible. Prove that breaking free from mediocrity isn't just a dream—it's a reality within reach.

Pay it forward. Build your legacy. And watch the cycle of abundance grow.

Conclusion

Level Up, One Step at a Time

You've made it to the end of this book, but the journey to leveling up your life is just beginning. Throughout these chapters, we've explored the mindset shifts, habits, and skills that can transform your life from financial mediocrity to extraordinary success. But let's take a moment to reflect on where you've been, where you are now, and where you're headed.

Recapping the Journey

We started by confronting the traps of average thinking and rewriting the money stories that held you back. You've learned the power of setting big, bold goals, mastering your mornings, and taking control of your time and priorities. You've explored how to develop financial habits for success, build resilience through discipline, and invest in yourself through continuous learning.

You've discovered the value of networking, creating multiple streams of income, and thinking long-term. And finally, you've explored the ultimate reward: thriving in financial freedom and giving back to create a ripple effect that extends beyond your own life.

Each chapter is a building block. Each step, no matter how small, has brought you closer to breaking free from mediocrity and moving toward a life of abundance, growth, and impact.

The Journey is Continuous

Leveling up isn't a one-time decision. It's not about quick fixes or overnight success. It's about showing up for yourself every day, committing to the habits and mindsets that propel you forward, and being willing to adjust as you grow.

There will be setbacks. There will be days when you feel stuck or unsure. But here's the truth: progress always beats perfection. Every small step forward, no matter how insignificant it feels in the moment, adds up to something extraordinary over time.

As long as you're moving, you're growing. As long as you're growing, you're leveling up.

Final Call to Action: The Next Step is Yours

Now comes the most important question: **What's your next step?**

Will you start tracking your spending? Set a bold financial goal? Wake up a little earlier tomorrow to win your day? Will you invest in a new skill, reach out to a mentor, or begin rewriting your money story?

You don't have to tackle everything at once. Start with one thing. Choose one habit, one mindset shift, or one small action from this book and commit to it today.

Your future self—the one thriving, excelling, and living with purpose—will thank you.

Dream Big, Take Action, and Thrive

Your life doesn't have to be defined by mediocrity. The potential to thrive financially, personally, and professionally is within you. It's not about where you started—it's about where you choose to go from here.

So take that first step. Believe in your ability to grow. Dare to dream bigger than you ever have before. And remember: the journey to leveling up is yours to create, one step at a time.

The next step is yours. Start today, and watch how far you can go.

Bonus Material 1
Action Plan Worksheets

These worksheets are designed to help you take the ideas from *Level Up* and turn them into actionable, trackable steps. Print them out or use them digitally—whatever works best for you. The key is to use them consistently and adjust as you grow.

---

1. Goal-Setting Template

Set clear, actionable goals for personal growth, financial success, and skill-building. Break them down into manageable steps to stay focused and track your progress.

Goal-Setting Template

Step 1: Define Your Goal

- What is your goal? Be specific:
  Example: Save $5,000 in one year.

Step 2: Why Does This Matter?

- Write down your "why."
  Example: To build financial security and reduce stress.

Step 3: Break It Down

- Identify the steps to achieve your goal:
    1. Calculate how much to save monthly ($417).
    2. Set up an automatic transfer for savings.
    3. Reduce expenses to free up $50 per month.

Step 4: Set Deadlines

- Assign target dates for each step:
  Example: Step 1 by [date], Step 2 by [date].

Step 5: Track Progress

- Create checkpoints to measure your success.
  Example: Check savings total every month.

---

2. Time-Blocking Template

Master your schedule by organizing your day around your priorities. Time-blocking ensures you focus on what matters most.

Time-Blocking Template

Time	Task or Activity	Priority Level
6:00 AM	Morning routine (gratitude, exercise, planning)	High
7:00 AM	Skill-building (online course, reading)	High
8:00 AM	Work-related tasks (focus project)	High
12:00 PM	Lunch break	Medium
1:00 PM	Networking (reach out, schedule calls)	Medium
3:00 PM	Side hustle work	High
6:00 PM	Family/personal time	Medium
9:00 PM	Reflect and plan for tomorrow	High

Tips for Success:

- Block high-priority tasks during your most productive hours.
- Keep distractions minimal during focus blocks.
- Leave room for breaks to stay energized.

3. Financial Tracking Worksheet

Track your income, expenses, and savings to take control of your finances. Awareness is the first step toward building wealth.

Financial Tracking Template

Category	Amount Budgeted	Amount Spent	Difference
Income			
Salary/Paycheck	$	$	$
Side Hustle Earnings	$	$	$
Other Income	$	$	$
Expenses			
Housing	$	$	$
Utilities	$	$	$
Groceries	$	$	$
Transportation	$	$	$
Entertainment	$	$	$
Miscellaneous	$	$	$
Savings			
Emergency Fund	$	$	$
Investments	$	$	$
Other Savings	$	$	$

Tips for Success:

- Review and update your worksheet weekly or monthly.
- Adjust your budget categories based on your goals and habits.

- Celebrate small wins, like sticking to your savings plan.

These worksheets are your tools for turning dreams into reality. Use them to stay focused, track progress, and make adjustments as needed. Remember: the key to leveling up is taking small, consistent steps—and these templates will help you do just that.

Bonus Material 2
Reflection Questions

These thought-provoking questions are designed to help you dig deeper into your mindset, habits, and goals. Use them as journaling prompts, conversation starters, or personal check-ins. Reflecting on these questions will help you identify areas for growth and create a clear path forward.

Habits and Mindset

1. What habits are currently holding you back from thriving?
2. When was the last time you stepped out of your comfort zone? What happened?
3. What limiting beliefs about money or success do you need to let go of?
4. How do you currently define financial freedom, and what does it look like for you?
5. What small change could you make today that would create a ripple effect in your life?

Goal Setting and Growth

6. What's the first skill or income stream you'll start building today?
7. If you could achieve any one financial goal this year, what would it be?
8. What's one area where you've settled for "good enough"? How could you improve it?
9. What's a big, bold goal you're afraid to admit but secretly want to pursue?
10. How will your life look different once you've achieved your financial dreams?

Time and Priorities

11. Are you spending your time in ways that align with your long-term goals? Why or why not?
12. What's one distraction you can eliminate to focus better on your priorities?
13. How can you reframe your daily routine to include more time for personal growth?
14. What's one task you've been procrastinating that would move you closer to success if completed?

Networking and Relationships

15. Who in your current network inspires you to level up? How can you spend more time learning from them?
16. What's one way you can add value to someone else's journey this week?
17. If you could have a mentor in any area of your life, who would it be and why?

Resilience and Gratitude

18. What's the biggest challenge you've overcome, and what did it teach you?
19. How do you handle setbacks? What could you do differently to bounce back faster?
20. What are three things you're grateful for today that help you move toward thriving?

Legacy and Giving Back

21. What legacy do you want to leave behind for your family and community?
22. How can you use your journey to inspire and mentor others?
23. If you achieved your version of success, how would you give back to those in need?

24. What impact do you want your life to have on the world around you?

These questions aren't just for pondering—they're a blueprint for self-discovery and action. Take time to answer them honestly, revisit them often, and let them guide you as you level up into the thriving life you deserve.

www.ingramcontent.com/pod-product-compliance
Lightning Source LLC
Chambersburg PA
CBHW070347230526
45471CB00006B/2460